Beginnings & Endings

BEGINNINGS AND ENDINGS

by
Paul Neumann

QUERCUS REVIEW PRESS
MODESTO, CA
2016

QUERCUS REVIEW POETRY SERIES, 2016
Sam Pierstorff, *Editor*

Published by Quercus Review Press
Department of English
Modesto Junior College
quercusreviewpress.com

QUERCUS
Review
P   R   E   S   S

Cover photo by Lisa M. Smith
Author photo by Doug Holcomb
Cover design by Sam Pierstorff
Book layout by Desiree Cervantes

Printed on acid-free paper
10 9 8 7 6 5 4 3 2 1

ISBN-13: 978-0692661529 (Quercus Review Press)
ISBN-10: 0692661522

Publications by Quercus Review Press (QRP) are made possible with the support of the Division of Literature & Language Arts at Modesto Junior College. A portion of the proceeds from the sale of this book will benefit creative writing scholarships.

For Pamela,
her loving-kindness and greatness of spirit.
She lives in every line.

TABLE OF CONTENTS

Part I - *Beginnings*

Part II - *Middle*

Part III - *Endings*

I

BEGINNINGS

*A series of poems written for my
granddaughter in the months before she was
born, as I began to understand that when
she was ten, I would be eighty-eight.*

1.

I call to you at the end of my life
and the very beginning of yours.
Soon, you will ask for stories,

the magic tales just at bedtime,
and I will spin the myths again,
mouth the time-worn words which

call you to sleep, to dream of maidens
wed to handsome princes in stone-built
castles wreathed in misty air

in a land where sun always shines,
dragons are always slain, and the
wicked never win. When you are

older, I hope, you will rewrite those
stories, turn them into your own
fables, fashion a different narrative.

All our lives are a fiction, little girl,
but you can choose how your story
will evolve, how within your myths

will live the mystery of your grown life,
where dragons will be fought with
your own power, not dependent

on a prince, however loving and
supportive, where you can leave your
castle, unafraid, and walk where

you will, through the vast and precious
world and the people you pass will
wonder at the brilliance of your passing.

2.

There will be time enough, I hope,
for me to come to know you,
to watch you start to understand

the margins of your life, time to
hear your first adventures into
language, time to hear you voice

your hopes and dreams and
shape them into the form
which will animate your life,

time to see how your mind will
inform the richness of your heart
and set you on a path that is

so compelling in its passion,
so focused on tomorrow that
you will never be humbled.

No time for the voices of those
who would teach you your place.

3.

Since my years with you will likely
not be long, surely ended by the time
you are fully grown and formed,

I often think what I would say to you
in a quiet moment as we walk the shore
at Carmel Beach, each of us lost

in the tidal rhythms of the building,
breaking waves, you at my side and
a wordless question for a moment

clouding the sunlight in your eyes,
asking not for answers but for insight,
for the snap of understanding.

How I wish a fragile bridge of words
could be there, spanning the years
between your young life and mine,

especially when questions loom
like fog on the horizon, and your
eyes are open and imploring.

But gray hair does not grant wisdom
and it may be that even my offered
words will not be enough to quell

the anguish that the young so deeply
feel, or find a way to loose the knots
that life so often ties, those tangles

which seem to lie in the very belly of
the empty zero which at times can be
the burden that later you must carry.

4.

It is winter in the valley, little girl,
fog hanging on the land, the water
of the San Joachin slow in the

channel, white rime on the rooftops
and crusty frost on the grass, as I
walk the dog in the early morning.

All this while, you rest in the warmth
of your mother's womb, suspended
in the fluid she provides, enclosed

in the quiet shelter of her body, but
slowly, in the flow of spring, the valley
will awake: the miracle of blossoms

in the orchards, the green birth of
leaves on the vines, and the slumbering
land will yawn in the soft rain and

come to life. So you in your cushioned
sleep will start to stir in the form your
father's seed, your mother's ovum, the

ecstasy of their fusing will have made.
Then you will enter with crinkled eyes
and ready mouth, eager for the possible.

5.

The streams of light which first will
        fill your eyes
bring bewilderment and wonder as
        the world beyond

your mother's arms is opened
        to your sight
and sense, the shapes and colors
        baffling and beguiling,

the odors ticking in your tiny nose
        like promises that
life will later keep, enticing, hopeful
        mysteries which

have no denotation or definition. Even
        in your mother's
arms you sense the presence of
        your father's

strength and tenderness; his fingers
        touch your face
and your tiny fingers hold his thumb.
        In his arms

you feel a shelter married to your
        mother's comfort,
the nurture of her breast, her steady
        heartbeat, and the

rhythm of her pulse, a cadence
       you have heard
for months, safe in her womb,
       the sanctuary

where conception first began. Later,
       you will come
to know the arrow of her will, the
       power in her

choices as your eyes open to the
       promise of tomorrow.

6.

These words I leave you are like footsteps
in the snow of understanding, faint marks,
leading to the rim of a sheer cliff, a dead

end to the path we keep and what we hope
to know: the profundity of our passage
in the world, the limit of our way ahead,

There are some who would tell you that
they know what lies beyond the mist
which hides the edge, that they know

how you can save yourself from falling
helpless in the air, like a leaf in the winter
wind, fluttering without purpose or provision,

their certainty a pale comfort except for
those who need abiding confirmation,
the good news proclaimed each Sunday

and the enfolding arms of faith, but you,
I hope, will see the path a different way,
embrace the shrouded mystery with all

your heart and mind and without fear
approach the verge and go to meet that
presence, knowing you will be welcome.

7.

Some would say the world that you
      will enter
is covered by a yellow haze, hanging
      like polluted air

above the valley foothills, sullen
      and brooding.
They say our world has lost its
      commitment

to civil values, that bonds no longer
      hold, that random
luxury runs rampant, and indolence
      infects the young,

addicted to ingenious possessions,
      wonders that
wizards create each year for their
      amusement. The old

will say there is no respect for custom
      or tradition and
declare the good world gone, lost
      to passing fancies.

All your life, little girl, you will hear those
      groans, the sullen
words of discontent, and it's not easy,
      when you're young,

to soar above the haze of jaded voices,
      confident that above
the sour sky will be a brilliant sun,
      ready for your eyes

8.

I see your future in the lives of seabirds:
the flight of pelicans as they graze the
surface of the sea, plunging down into
the depths to capture what the ocean
might disclose; the skitter of scoters,
dashing in and out of the waves, their
long beaks finding the buried sand crabs;
the scatter of gulls turning through the
light, searching the air and then settling
on the sand of the river mouth, at ease
in the company of others.

                        When your
world has opened to a future which is firm
and flexible, I will not be here to witness,
but I know, in this dream of language and
possibility, that you will find a purpose
to satisfy the hunger that is your birthright.
Like the seabirds drawn to the vast
mystery of the ocean, so you will find
a place in the rich mosaic of even ordinary
life from which to search fearlessly and
embrace your arrival.

9.

My sense is that, when grown, you
          may have to bear
the sometimes heavy weight of beauty,
          the burden of green

eyes and icy words, even in a circle
          of friends who
smile their envy at the entitlement
          you seem to wear

so effortlessly, the looks you draw, the
          hush when you
enter a room, the pleasure of others
          in your presence.

Your mother's Grecian profile, your
          father's virile maturity
can form an exotic loveliness attractive
          to those people

who worship a cosmetic beauty
          and hover around
the flower, buzzing and sultry at the
          scent of sensuality

heavy in the air and ever stronger
          as you age.
Beauty must be borne with grace
          and thoughtful care,

so be mindful of your mother and your
          grandmother who
spurned the facile charm of flattery
          and shallow vanity.

10.

Perhaps this storm will clear the air,
my mother used to say, when a
shadow was lying on her heart.

Her faith absolved the fallen, the
lust that swallowed every lure, even
forgave the darker chapters in her

nation's past: the clank of chains,
the trail of tears, the horror of bombs
all assumed in His infinite will.

Like her, little girl, all these are your
birthright, and while these clouds
darkened the air, the country went about

its business and prayed in my mother's
church on Sunday and the storm has
never come to clear the shadows.

11.

The Parable of the Good Samaritan is worth
much more than pious platitudes, mouthed from
the pulpits of rivulet churches which trickled
away from the great stream of early christianity.
The wounded traveler was a stranger, not one
of their own, so the righteous priest and his
companion passed him by, pressed by other
needs, no thoughts given to the coonbeanerkike
who lay bleeding on the hard ground.

How easy it is to help one of our own and
how difficult to aid one of the others, a menacing
shadow, fearsome, wrapped in danger. Not like us.
The Samaritan stopped. What deeper message
could the parable convey? There will be some
moments, little girl, when your goodness will be
challenged at the fork of a road, and you will have
to choose a turn which may darken the rest of your
days or fill them with light.

12.

Talk is the coinage of the old, and they
          spend it freely,
stories about the moments in their lives
          with the world
at their feet, and everything was possible,
          tales retold
and shaped to fit the fiction which has
          become the
woven fabric of their lives, tailored into
          parables which
they think will teach the lessons they
          have learned
so the young will know their value

When the stories are told well and not
          repeated just
for ego's sake, when the listeners are
          allowed a moment
of reflection or engagement, a way
          to enter the stories
and extend them, then the fiction can
          sew generations
together with the thread of wisdom.
          Words to live by,
my mother used to say as she knitted
          her own life
into patterns learned from her mother.

13.

Some people may tell you that your path
through life, little girl, must be uncluttered
and defined or you will never achieve
what they imagine you should do, and
they will talk of plans, the right schools,
career choices, and say that you will
need to know your goals and how to meet
them, the earlier the better, for success
or even happiness.

Peace, strength of mind and heart, integrity,
finding a balance, all these cannot be parsed as
objectives but as a way of life to be found, if
you are fortunate, followed and never bargained
for praise and profit. Look, the finches in my garden
fly at random in the air, then settle on the seed bag
where they perch and peck, each bird approaching
at its own direction, sharing only the urge for seed,
such a simple and sustaining hunger and all they
know or need, no matter how scattered their
approach to the bag.

14.

A glass of wine, a loaf of country bread, the wealth
of butter, fresh fish grilled with a pinch of salt,
a lemon wedge or two, followed by some fruit. All
my life, little girl, I have taken comfort in simple food,
carefully cooked. Eat, my father used to say, eat, drink
and talk with people whom you love. Share the supper,
if you can, but even alone taste the ocean depths in
the fish, the richness of earth in the grains of bread,
the old wood of the fruit tree, the divine blessing of
the vine. All I could wish for you is here on this antique
table, with friends and family gathered for this covenant
with the simple truth of food: the smell, the taste, in
hand-turned bowls and plates, elemental in its humble
elegance.

15.

My father was a boy in frozen Poland
when one icy Christmas day, the heavens
opened and a miracle orange dropped
into his hands, the first he had ever seen,
as if an alien planet, a wink in the winter
sky, had burst into flower and fruit and
blessed him with an abundance he
had never known or thought about. Such
miracles, little girl, are always a matter
of perspective. In your life you will know
many marvels, the fruit of a country whose
bounty would be a wonder for my father,
as foreign as his birthplace became,
its poverty and hunger. His challenge was
always just to eat, stay warm and safe,
while yours will be to house the accidental
affluence of your life.

              Could my father see
that apparition coming? Could he know how
a simple fruit could change his life? When
that orange first appeared, with all its citric
mystery, he knew he had to run toward
a different future, leaving the cold mud and
meager scraps of dry potatoes, so he left on foot,
with only the clothes on his back, hoping for
another miracle, and made his way, finally,
to America, a castaway on a foreign shore.
No language. No money.

Little girl, you
will have no knowledge of your great grand
father other than these lines on fading paper
which you may find some day forgotten in
a disused drawer, and you will wonder how
this man could survive without the comforts that
surround you. If I am still alive when you
chance to read these words, I will tell you that
life can be a journey from miracle to miracle,
if your eyes are open and not drugged by opulence,
and that wonder may be born from something humble
like an orange.

16.

In the painting by Rembrandt, the prodigal
kneels in the encircling arms of his father,
feels the embrace of lightness, the older
brother shadowed in the background,
his face indistinct, his presence un-noted.
For the father, forgiveness is easy; the
soft rain of gratitude melts the cold snow
and the meltwater runs to the river, finally
down to the deep sea, the profound depths
of parental love.

     But the elder brother---
what of him? In the Sierra some snow can
remain in crevices in the granite, ice-bound
even through the heat in midsummer. Can he
suffer the loss of wealth so carelessly wasted
while he labored---and yet have faith in his
father's love? Some questions, little girl,
are not easily answered, but forgiveness requires
the grace to accept love as greater than gain.
That much we know.

17.

While you are living, little girl,
if you are sensitive to suffering,
aware of injustice that haunts
the world, then the harmony of
your life will be altered, and
you will feel for the desperate
who cling to hope while the
powerful control their lives.

The simple-minded will say that
ignorance is bliss, best to turn
your head and avoid the sight of
human misery. Why concern
yourself with those who are helpless
in their need? Nothing can be done.

Solutions, of course, can be hard
to find, but to try, to act, to push
against the stone not only out of pity
or empathy, is to fully live. Arendt
wrote that the actions of just one
humanist, pushing against the
hell of Nazi Germany, was enough to
affirm hope in the human condition.

Be one of those, open-eyed.

18.

Driving in the hills beyond Arezzo, the car
on a single, rutted track, following the map
the innkeeper scrawled. No lights. No signs.
At every curve we thought to stop, but no room
to turn and a gaping ditch on either side,
so we kept on in the dark, gripped by doubt,
distrusting the crude map.

                                        Then we
rounded a corner, saw lights, heard the music
from the trattoria, and found a footpath from
the carpark to the door. On each table, a menu
we could not translate but with some familiar
words, so pasta con coniglio, we said to the
frowzy woman who took the order and shouted
to the cooks in the kitchen.

                                   If you ever travel to
Arezzo, little girl, you'll ride in a car with GPS,
no scrawled map needed. There would be no
anxiety, no indecision and the rutted track
would now be paved, with signage every mile,
the trattoria morphed into a fine restaurant,
adventure scrubbed from the experience. All
risk removed. Sheltered and safe.

                                     The pasta we ate
that coal black night so many years ago, the rabbit
in a creamy sauce on fetucini with some grated
parmigiano, was flavored with gratitude, graced
with relief from the fear which followed us up the
hillside. We made our way back to Bagorno, still
tasting a meal flavored with meaning, seasoned
by the tangled knots of chance and reward.

19.

In the country of the old, little girl,
stories are told again and again:
how the bells tolled when war
was declared, how people danced
in the streets when peace came to be.
Of course, there were no bells, no
dancing, just the yellow light of the
radio dial, the mournful sound of the
refrigerator closing, the smell of father's
cigarette as he smoked in the dark.

In the country of the old, anger is a
province often visited: loss of control,
nagging pains and always the grim
specter of being irrelevant, unnoticed
in the corner of the room, a voice
drowned out by the thunder of new
ideas, styles and electronic devices.
No patience for old stories, no matter
how artfully told. The past is gone,
there is little future and so just anger.

20.

In the intricate fabric of your genes,
little girl, there is a thread of Southern
gentility, as finely fashioned as lace,
fragile as the Belleek cups your great
grandmother used for tea with the friends
who would call on a sultry Alabama
afternoon, the honoring of respect
and tradition, head high, back straight,
courteous and careful never to cross
the limits of good taste, the early
evening light falling on plates of cucumber
sandwiches and petit fours, the ladies
sitting quietly, wearing white gloves.

Some would say that such a culture
could not last, that such formality must
yield to a less structured way of life, and
so it has. You will never host an afternoon
visit, the silver tea service will stand like
a relic on the sideboard, collecting dust,
and you'll meet your friends in a coffee shop
or a wine bar after work. But the foundation
of gentility, I hope, will still survive in you,
in your gracious spirit, so much more meaningful
than manners, and when you reach out to
a person in need, offer help to a friend, you
will do so with your great grandmother's
fingers, no longer governed by white gloves.

21.

When I was small, I roamed alone the coast
below the mansion where my father worked
during the war. Some days a roar of waves
rushed up the rocks where I would climb, and
I was cautious with the angry water, but excited
by the risk of the churning forces.

        On those stormy
winter nights, my mother showed me how to read
fables and tales, quickened the blood of my
young imagination so I could feel the edge of
exotic ideas, the taste of adventure, the deep
ocean of my hidden, unformed life.

        And why,
little girl, am I telling you this? There were
cypress trees on the cliff edge that were bent
by the force of the wind, unable to grow as freely
as they might. I walked where I wanted, dreamed
my own dreams, unafraid of the world that was open
before me. So it will be for you.

22.

The year you were born, the valley
was dry and fields gone fallow.
Little rain fell. Thin snow in the Sierra.
Fear in the air after three years of drought.
Jobs dried up as well.

In the week before you were born,
another crazed killing in California.
Wars continuing in Syria, Afghanistan.
Senseless violence in the Middle East
between Shia and Sunni.

The night you were born was fertile
with promise. You were so tiny. A wink
of lucidity. A drop of water. A grain of
sand in the war-burnt desert. Your
small hand holding the tip of my finger.

The reservoirs refilling.

.

II

MIDDLE

Patterns

My wife used patterns learned
from her mother, from other
generations, to knit the lives
of our children, but as they aged,
she was less strict about directions
she had once followed so religiously,
counting stitches, marking each
carefully on paper.

        The wool still
slides through her fingers, but now
the needles click in complex rhythms,
and the sweater or scarf may take
a surprising shape. Oh well, she
would say, as long as it keeps them
warm, what matter an irregular row
or a dropped stitch or two.

        As our
children grew, they were not always
what we had meant them to be, so we
had to grow as well, learning new
patterns for ourselves to follow, no
longer trying to knit the children in
a fixed design, but allowing for their
changes, however strange the ways
they found to keep warm.

Birth and Renewal

When the baby was born, a hole
in our hearts, caused by the loss of
a child, was filled, the blessing
of the birth so healing that it filled
us with joy, and we found the courage
to love another generation, though
wounded, as a woman can suffer
the pain of childbirth and still desire.

When a child becomes a stranger,
a dark void opens, and a dull ache
throbs in the heart, though the loss
is an absence, not the snap of mortality.
Still, a part of the family goes missing,
and the wound still quickens with each
real or imagined slight, as the child moves
further and further away.

When little Mary appeared, and her tiny
life began our renewal, I thought of that
other Mary who knew only the wonder
of the birth, in her innocence unaware of
how the harmony of the world would be
restored, all trespasses forgiven, that lepers
would be made clean, cripples could walk
and lost children returned.

Nurse Logs

It poured all day as we hiked a
trail in the rain forest, leaving the
warmth of the dry hotel, but wanting
a walk through the green and verdant
wild. "Viriditis," Hildegard* called it,
after she emerged from the bleak
solitude of her cell in the cloister,
the green force that fires the world.
She had never seen such growth,
never felt the texture of leaves or
the roughness of bark. never saw
new shoots struggling up through
soil toward the sun. All this she had
to imagine, this virginal bride of Christ,
confined in the austere monastery,
in dreams which found life in her words
and paintings. What mysteries might
have been revealed had she seen
the nurse logs lying on the forest floor,
young seedlings growing from the fertile
body of the fallen tree, seen the green
power being born again in the massive
trunk lying in a bed of rotting limbs and
decaying leaves.

The woman I was with
became my wife, a bright green shoot
growing from the body of two dead marriages.
The force of our love was fierce and verdant,
all that Hildegard, virginal bride of Christ,
might have known in her most wanton
dreams.

As the sensual can be born
out of solitude, as passion might live in the
solitude of a cloistered cell, so life may be
birthed from death, love from the absence
of it. We left the forest, soaked with rain,
found our hotel and fell into bed.

*Hildegard was a twelfth century mystic, offered to
God by her parents at the age of eight.*

Magdalene

When the prostitute came before Christ,
she washed his feet with tears of remorse
and dried them with her unbound hair.
His compassion enfolded her, and acceptance
made her whole.

Outside the small house belonging to Simon,
the wind brushed the branches of the olive
trees and turned the color of the leaves,
as if arranging a new possibility, a merciful
balance as yet unknown.

Lost in the background were the pious guests,
bound by convention and the law, shocked
that the Messiah, knowing the uncleanliness
of the woman, would not keep himself apart
from an untouchable.

Now we know that the world had turned,
that power no longer prevailed.

Homeless

The park is a place of green and light,
trees softening the fierce summer sun,

sheltering the homeless who sit on the
benches, lie on the grass, their shopping

carts filled with clutter, green trash bags
holding the things that matter. What a

shame, people say when they see them
in a place meant for children playing,

lovers lying on the grass and old men
walking their dogs. Something should

be done, they say; this litter removed,
the area restored. The park was not meant

for them and their scrawny dogs, the harsh
jangle of their unwashed bodies: drunks

and druggies with no place to go; nothing
to do; unsettled, unwanted; no use. But in

the eye of your mind, as you pass by the
park, you might see a force brighter than

sunlight, wandering among the people and
each turns wordlessly toward the aura of light.

We know this is impossible, that divine
solutions do not occur, but the deep urge

for an answer would tear at the heart if
these people were one of us, but of course

they are the other.

Misery

I.

While some pain can be agonizing,
a sharp burst which blasts the nerves
and stuns the senses, misery often
lies in small discomforts: drops of
rain on a neck bare in the cold,
the trickle of water seeping under
a threadbare coat.

Most mundane is the need to spill
the gut-waste, squat and grunt,
in a crowd, in the meadow where
the others rest. No way to be alone.
So a public shame of stench, eyes
everywhere, staring. No disgrace
more shameful.

II.

The great tide of refugees flows from
where they were, the agony of killing,
to where they might be, fed by a flicker
of possibility, the chances of death in a
rickety boat better than the slaughter of
barrel bombs.

They wait quietly by the side of the road,
thousands of them, faceless and hungry,
while water and food are handed out.
If they were to look just beyond the
chain-link fence lining the road, they
might see a woman with a clutch of
hens, a man hoeing a plot of ground,
ready for seed.

III.

It is all so ordinary, this vision. They have
lived this dream in Syria, many lifetimes
ago and now have left the agony behind.
What's left is misery: a small sip from a
cold cup, a freeze-dried meal on a plastic
tray. No warmth or shelter. No rest. The
screeching hag of anxiety, the sniffling
of children.

Skellig Michael*

Toward Skellig Michael, the monks rowed out
on a favoring tide, the North Sea beating
on the hide-covered corracles. Landing on
the island, a rocky finger reaching skyward,
they built a slate hut for each, and there they
stayed, gruel-fed, warmed only with animal skins.
Theirs was a simple place where prayer
could be made and commitment tested, an
urge to find God in their solitude, rarely meeting,
it is said, or conversing, lost in the lonely and
rigorous search for the spirit, their lives a severe
burden of cold beauty, too difficult for us to carry,
but in silence they found strength and sacrificed
the soft voices of friends for the call of circling
seabirds and the exacting journey toward the soul.

* Skellig Michael is a rocky island 11k south of Ireland

Wonder

for Sage

He spins the golden wedding ring on the table,
flicks his fingers and the circle is a blur of movement,
whirling, whirring as it turns so quickly, then
clatters to the wooden surface.

The little girl is sitting in her chair at the table,
fascinated by the spinning, even when it stops,
and he slips the ring back on his finger: her father,
inviting the wonder of the child.

Her eyes are filled with this miracle, this flow of light.
Transfixed, she does not reach her hands to touch
the golden blur. Just to see is to engage, to fill her
mind with magic. She looks to her father

when the whirring stops, holds his eyes, this agent
of amazement, creator of a new form of glow and a
rare moment of motion, all by the snap of his fingers.
Abracadabra. The world that awaits her.

Lazarus and Laffler*

In the parable, Lazarus sits under the table
where the rich man eats and waits for the
scraps to fall from the lavish meal, a benefit
he is granted but not entitled to, for he can be
driven away by the dogs or denied his place
by the man's retainers should he be too bold,
demand more than his crusts and bits.
The rich man's name is not given, nor how
he made his fortune. He might be a venture
capitalist, a hedge fund manager or CEO
of a corporation. All we are told is the luxury
of his table, the abundant wealth of food,
enough that he can afford the welfare of the
leavings which sustain Lazarus, scrambling
on his knees in his place beneath the table.

*Arthur Laffler was the proponent of "trickle down"
economics, the theory that the lower and middle
classes would ultimately benefit from the prosperity
of the powerful and wealthy.

Work and Toil

There, in the city, so many forms of
work: the tedium of an office, the cold
calls trolling for business, hypnotic
glow of the computer screen, drudgery
of a desk, papers shuffled on the surface.
In box. Out box. Summer and winter.
Indoor labor, daily routine, the monotony
of facts and figures, the dull burden of
authority, difficult decisions, hiring and
firing. But clean hands.

Toil? Another
matter. Out on the ranches and farms,
picking, pruning, weeding, bent over
the hoe. Sweat in the eyes, dirt under
fingernails and ground into callouses.
Never come clean. But bearable, so the
spark of life can live. Men slouched in
the parking lot at Walmart, hoping for
a day shouldering the burden of the sun,
the misery of dust. Never clean. An ache
deep in the muscles and bones. But
provision for the beast.

Anything to feed the beast.

Fault Lines

Selfishness.

Mine because it lives in me, a remora
sucking on a shark, a leech swimming in blood.
A need which blots out every other, an appetite
which must always be met. The homeless man
squatting on the hot air vent in winter, the cripple
with his cane. They have made their own way.
I need not see them.

Elitism.

Above the rest, above the rabble, lifted
by the winds of insecurity above the smell of sweat,
like a desperate balloon, thin-skinned, fragile,
floating over sewage. Never crude behavior at
the dinner table. White damask, sterling silver,
crystal goblets. I am not the other, never them.
So fearful that I could be.

Greed.

A golden coin thrown into the gaping maw
whistles as it falls, makes no noise when it hits
the bottom. The hunger in the emptiness needs
more and more. No end.

The Sargasso Sea

In the ocean of consciousness, we live on the surface,
waves of wives and children breaking on the rocky shore of
expectations and failed experiences, inspiration and expiration,
the tidal rhythms of occupations, purpose, ambitious dreams
of power and wealth that ran aground, and sunlight was once
a gilded path of possibility gliding out to the horizon. Far below,
out in the limitless deep, lies the Sargasso Sea, a knot of kelp,
of flotsam and jetsam, the detritus of our psychic lives, an
unconscious tangle beneath the surface, so difficult to unsnarl
that we live with it, fearful of its disclosure, never revealing its
presence, even to lovers, family or friends, a gnarl suspended
in the gyre of the spirit that we choose not to visit. So often, we
find ourselves caught in that underwater sea and never move,
no matter wind or wave or flux of current, becalmed by apathy,
the fear of what the underworld might disclose, a captive with
so little time left to face the wonder life has offered and then
withdrew.

Martha and Mary

Martha and Mary. Upstairs, Downstairs:
Social banter in the drawing room;
the cook finishing the pudding for desert;
dinner upstairs with all its stateliness:
the good silver, stiff collars, starched shirt;
floured arms and hands around the common
table below, drinking tea after the formal
meal has been served; General Haig over port,
justifying the slaughter at the Somme with
serious men in waistcoats: talk of unfortunate
casualties, reinforcements on the way.
Mary and Martha. In cottages in Shropshire,
clenched hands around the table; hunger and
ration cards; Billy called up. At the Somme,
troops marching against the machine guns;
generals planning another assault: that vital
hill, four hundred yards, ten thousand deaths
away, so the whistle and over the top.
No time to ponder questions asked in drawing
rooms, as serious men sip the last of the pre-war
port. "Barnes, there's been a spill," Martha
and Mary.

One enriched by the Messiah's presence,
hanging on every word from the divine stranger.
The other? A cleaner, a scrubber who tidies up.
Belongs downstairs. Needed there.

After the Storm

After the storm, the drenching release
in the drought-stricken valley, the clouds
moved slowly east toward the Sierra where
the rain turned to snow and ice on the slopes,
blurring the sharp outlines, and the peaks
blazed in fierce winter light, clear even as
I walked, fifty miles away, down in the valley.
There, the trees were stripped of leaves,
the fiery colors of Pistache and Liquid Amber
now mulched in the wet streets, and I thought
of death, how the fierce passion of life dims,
as always, when the great cycle turns. We plant,
we reap, then the fields turn fallow. Soon, the
winter sky becomes cloudy and the rains begin,
softening the soil so the new seeds can seek
the light. What else is there to learn?

Beach House

From the deck of the rented beach house,
I can turn my eyes through the wave-mist
and envison another world, thousands
of miles west, with limitless possibilities
beyond the horizon, in the dreamy stillness
of a restful afternoon, my laptop quiet on the
coffee table, briefcase closed for this weekend
away. In the rise and fall of the swell beyond
the deck, a lone egret fishes from a raft of kelp,
its long beak darting down below the surface
of the water, searching the limitless depths,
while my mind soars over the sea toward
the possible, "going where the eyes take you,"
as the proverb reads.

If I turn east, toward the Pajaro Valley,
acres upon acres of artichoke fields, close
behind the beach house, and the forms of
workers, almost invisible in the mist, swaddled
in sweat clothes, weeding, thinning, picking
and then packing the artichokes for shipment:
a line of portable toilets on the edge of the field
and a cluster of old cars parked for the end of a long day.
The faces of the workers have been bent toward
the earth and the end of one furrow, the beginning
of another, row after row, day after day, their long
hoes searching steadily in the dirt, turning the dark
clods of the alluvial soil left by the drainage
of the Salinas River.

And where should
my eyes take me, as I stand on the damp deck
with a cup of espresso and a warm croissant,
petrale sole and an artichoke later for dinner?

Tidal Life

In the lagoon, still silence, the water calm
and unruffled, rafts of kelp moving with the
rhythm of the brackish ripples, gulls and
pelicans fluttering on the water, rising for
a moment, then falling back and breaking
the surface, briefly interrupting the quiet.

Beyond the sand bar, waves build and break,
wash the sloping sand, then flow back to
the heaving ocean where ghostly swells
begin, making their steady way to shore
then rising, cresting when they meet a rocky
shelf beneath the surface.

We live our lives in tidal rhythms, rising and falling.
Inspiration fills us with the sweet air of possibility,
and we hold our breath as long as we can, lungs
filling and releasing, never stopping or slowing
until finally gone and we expire, a wavelet
foaming on the sand before returning to the
deepest water.

Summer Sun

The summer sun is not a friend to older men,
      and we wither in its heat,
but in the early morning on the urban trail,
      I walked through
memories of the fog in Berkeley, where each day
      I tried to read
the crumpled map that marked my life, hoping
      to find another way.
There was little sun on those grey days, only
      a persistent mist,
clinging to the trees and dampening the streets.
      I was lost in
lectures and books, trying to "make something
      of myself," as my mother
would say, but without an idea which path
      I should take or
what it was I might make. Then, still unsure,
      I came to the sun
in the great valley, a young man who found he
      could stand in
the fierceness of the light and glow with promise.

Spain and Spain

The tourist brochures say Torremolinos,
once a sleepy fishing village, now welcomes
the pale Europeans who flock to the sun
each spring and escape the dreary rainfall
of their grimy cities. They are lured by the
fantasy of topless beaches, roulette in
the casino, boozy parties with friends and
family, offered a package tour for two weeks
on the Costa del Sol, leaving behind the rut
of dead end jobs and grey row houses.

                                    We
lived for a time in a small village seven miles
above the coast called Mijas, happy to have
the blue Mediterranean far below our patio,
walked the quiet streets, ate bouquerrones
with gazpacho in a small bodega, enriched
that plain meal with a bottle of Valdepenas,
so inexpensive that Alberto would not let me
buy a glass, "Drink what you want," he would
say, as he brought the bottle. In the plaza
each day the buses brought tourists searching for
the soul of Andalusia or a tee-shirt for Alfie
back home.

Drought

Here, in the valley, the water runs slowly
in the channels of the rivers, no wildflowers
grow on the sides of the trail, only a straggle
of yarrow, a clotted clump of poppies, and
even the grasses are flattened by the sun,
a yellow mat of shrivelled straw.

                    Year after year
the drought has continued, water turned to a
trickle in the irrigation canals, old ruins exposed
in the cracked bottoms of the reservoirs as the
lakes slowly recede, eroded walls of buildings,
abandoned towns where the faith of past lives
was rewarded by rainfall and snow.

                    The worst
prayer was a plea, as whispers began, farmers slept
fitfully, and neighbors raised yard signs---Pray
For Rain: 1 Thessalonians---watched for answers
to appear in the empty skies: dark clouds and
showers of mercy, but none came.

                    The best
people I know are prayerful, at peace with the
seasonal flow of time's slow breathing. They know
this drought is a mote in the eye of the centuries.
No prayer, no matter how fervent, will turn
the hands of the clock, the rivers continue to create
their own channels, and the rains may someday
fall.

My Father and the War

Every month the letters arrived from the
old country with desperate requests
for the man in America, the gossamer
thread still twitched by the family, thin
cries from the forsaken, hopeless and
heart-breaking for he could do nothing.
An ocean between them, after he had
escaped, an ocean of understanding and
experience once he had landed and
made his new home. So the letters
stayed in a bureau drawer and called
to him in the night, he in one twin bed,
my mother in the other. Could she hear
those cries? Certainly she never eased
his anguish with the warmth of her body,
as I came finally to understand, so he lived
alone with the guilt and sorrow, knowing
he would never see them again, lost souls
in the barren waste of eastern Germany,
even after the war was over, and the terror
of those last years came through the yellow
eye of the radio.

Paris

In Paris, in the Bois de Boulogne, we would
sit and watch old couples on the benches,
silent, looking back on the scenes of their lives:
young lovers lying on the grass, pressed against
each other, her hair undone: a businessman taking
his lunch, newspaper folded, tie loosened, cheese
on a baguette, relished with the luxury of time
slowly spent.

We're in Paris, we would say, the City of Light,
and the trees glowed with a vibrant green,
shifting and changing as the wind stirred the leaves
and ruffled the placid water of the pond, small ripples
on the smooth surface. There, in the park, so easy
to see magic in everywhere we walked, miracles
in the people we watched, the fantasy we had longed
for in California, so many miles ago.

Back home, in a week, the dream began slowly to
fade when our usual routines began in our small city,
a place without glitter or mystery, Paris having vanished.
"Back to reality," we said. Then, on the urban trail on
an early morning walk, birdsong and wildflowers blooming,
a Russian woman stopped and gave me a part of the
miracle of her life, poems written with a magic hand,
and the trees glowed.

Seasons

There are those who say there are no seasons
in the valley, only sun and wind, fog and cold.
no endings and beginnings, just gradual changes
within the margins of the weather: temperatures
growing warmer, then colder, but a cloudless sky.
at times, in the grip of winter, a sharp wind in
spring, early rainfall in June, cold clouds interrupting
a golden autumn. No drama.

　　　　　　　　And those people want
the theatrical: a drive to Yosemite and the massive
bulk of El Capitan: thunderous waves on the coast.
We're in the middle, people like to say, between
mountains and ocean, only a short journey to a place
to hold the dying eye and mind, a trip to talk about,
somewhere entertaining. Meaning is not in things,
but in between, others might say, in an intersection
like home, the heartland, a valley blessed with sun
and water where people can stay, not wander off
to find joy and diversion.

　　　　　　　　The longing of the ashen
self for meaning, inspiration, can only be sustained
through the knowledge of a place, however modest,
where godlight shines in every weather

Some Consolation

The lagoon is quiet
in the evening light, the sand bar
blocks the thundering winter ocean,
and the placid river flows into the marsh
where sea birds float and smoooth their
feathers in the open water among the
reeds and sedge.

Where has the time
gone? we used to say when the hours
would pass so quickly, years filled with
jobs, children, the tension of busy lives,
but now, in the still water, small ripples
move the surface of the water, and even
the wind is pensive.

When we are young,
our eyes are drawn to the drama of the ocean,
the fierce currents running, waves breaking,
exploding on the rocky shore in a fury of
movement: so much energy, such little
pause or patience.

Then, as the end is near, the quiet lagoon.

Simple Soup and Michelangelo's David

In Florence, we walked to l'Accademia late
one afternoon, entered just before the doors
closed, found the darkened gallery lined
with unfinished figures struggling out of the
marble blocks. Then, irresistably, our eyes
were held by the massive form of David at rest,
his face content, his glance pensive, the one
hand with the sling relaxed but the tension
of the conflict with Goliath somehow living
silently in the marble, and we bore the burden
of the statue, the marriage of stone and spirit
that inspired a hunger which was so complex
it could not be shared.

                              As children,
we are taught the story of David and Goliath.
So much at stake. The stone is thrown, the giant
falls, and good has triumphed over evil. The drama
fulfills us through its simplicity and finality, but
the statue took us further, in a feast of emotion
and sense we could not digest, and so we left
the gallery stunned but unsatisfied, each lost
in wordless thought.

                              Later, in a
small trattoria near Ponte Vecchio, we ordered
Zuppa di Polpette with a loaf of crusty bread and
a bottle of full-bodied Barolo. Before we ate, a walk
through the piazza in front of San Croce, sun setting
beyond the bulk of the Duomo, the wonder of
the day leaving us still hungry, dazed by godlight,
so we spooned the soup, broke the bread and drank
the wine, finally satisfied by simpler tastes.

III

ENDINGS

Fog

In summer, fog hung in cypresses and pines
on the coast where I was raised. "Pea Soup,"
my father used to call it when it blotted out
the shape of the ocean, even hid the boulders
below our house. He still did some work:
weeding, pruning, raking the wet leaves,
holding on to the habits of his life with fingers
weak and frail, but then he became lost in
the thickening mist, a ghostly form in the grey,
and we took no further journeys of the spirit
together, father and son, hand in hand by
the ocean. There were only the dark depths
of the chasm, which I could not see, where
something of himself was still breathing,
jabbering in a whirl of words I could not follow.

His was a fog even deeper than dementia,
not just the absence of memory or the loss
of purposeful movement. At the end only
 his mouth opening like a bird when the spoon
was offered, but no appetite left, just the
hunger of a body holding a wisp of life.

Deadfalls

for my mother

In the worst places there are none:
trees logged, slash cut, the scarred
ground cleared, debris dragged away,
new seedlings planted. Forest Science.
Occasionally, in the foothills or the
deep unmanaged forests you will find them:
scarred by lightning, sapped by disease,
finally windswept to the ground,
roots flung higher than the fallen trunk.
Then the carpenter ants and termites
begin their work, scavenging, cleaning
the skeleton, white fingers of limbs stark
against the brown grasses and pine needles.
Then the bulk of the tree settles slowly,
season by season into the rain-softened ground
and returns to the earth.

When you see these deadfalls, you will know
the form that death should follow: jagged bolt
in a weakened heart, last fall in a familiar place,
then the years gradually erasing the memories.
Finally, the communion with all fallen lives and
the aura of the earth.

Fear of Falling

For the old, no fear quite like the
fear of falling. A fractured wrist,
elbow or shoulder are the cost one pays
to soften the drop, ease the shock
at the sudden loss of control.

Some deep core is shaken when
we trip. A confused tangle of knees,
arms, legs, then the frantic struggle to
get up, reclaim our place, brush aside
the offered help.

Even though we old ones shuffle,
eyes on the ground, being so careful,
a mere crack in the sidewalk, rough fold
of a rug, can tear the fragile fabric
of balance.

So little left now to manage. The
gardener mows the lawn, the wife does
the shopping, cooks the meals, pays
the bills. The children visit but never
seem to need advice.

The survival of dignity means the most.
An upright body, moving at our will,
hides the other failings, covers the slow
erosion of the self and with such little
time left before the final fall.

Blather

It is said that the old are wise,
that they have sorted and stored
their experience, that the wisdom
of their years has been centered
on the wheel. The summer heat
has passed, and a cooling autumn
wind rustles the branches of the trees,
the streets near the houses silent
as night prepares to fall. In that
quiet time, stories from the past
can be told, with thoughts that can
capture the mind of an eager child.
Through parables and spoken codes,
the legacy of a full life can be passed
to another generation, but wisdom
must have a willing ear and can be lost
in the chatter of texts and tweets,
the idle babble of uncaring children.
Neglect can quicken the desperate need
of the old to fill the quiet air, even with
idle talk, anything to claim again a place
in the circle, to matter.

So then---blather.

Pain in Old Age

It is true old age is marred by pain,
the ache of muscles seldom used,
and sharper pangs of spinal spasms
or damaged nerves, so I look for a
chair where my bones can rest at last,
and I think of the old ones, the ancianos,
sitting in the plaza, in Mijas, bent from
labor in the fields, hands gnarled like
grape vines, faces lined and worn,
dressed in Sunday black with a white
shirt and a hat like the one my father
never used, here in his new country,
a survival, stored deep in his closet
like a memory, and with the hat a
feathered band, thousands of stitches
binding the gold-flecked feathers to
the muslin, a decoration for a special
day which never came, but when he
left the weathered house in Poland, left
the frozen fields scoured by winter winds,
he took the hat as if he knew a day would
come when he would wear it on a plaza,
sitting with the other old ones,
prosperous and proud, welcomed in their
company, but that day never came.

Archaeology

Even in a family there are few who ask
the old to tell the buried stories of their lives.
Some shards remain, visible on the surface,
easily observed, but the deepest sites require
patience and a curious mind. Excavation is
not easy, especially when fragile remnants
survive but must be brought up intact, the old soil
carefully brushed away so that the memory can
be fully exposed in the sunlight and recovered,
even after all these years.

      Why bother? Some
would say. Long lives should end in peace,
the balm of forgetfulness better than the possible
pain of disclosure, but the old need to open
their lives to the young. When a generation is
cast aside in silence, stories are lost, and the aged
feel they have been discarded. It is never easy
for lives to be uncovered, for the tomb to be
opened, but only then can they appear, eyes open
like Lazarus, to tell what they have seen.

The Limit of Technology

The Fitbit that I wear on my belt
     when I walk
or run has a mystical display with
     alchemical designs
and algorhythmic wizardry, so
     when I press
a button, it shows me how many
     miles I have
gone, how high I have climbed,
     and how many
calories I have burned. Press the
     button three times,
and a flower appears. The more
     I exercise, the
longer the stem, so I try each day
     to lengthen
my flower, grow my health and life.

What my Fit-Bit does not display
     is how many
miles I still have to travel or the day
     of my death.

Tattoos

People my age are put off by tattoos.
How strange, they say, why do they do it?
Sleeves, chains, hearts pierced by an arrow,
names of lovers, belief in Christ, love for
mother, all preserved in inked patterns,
secrets of the heart, open to the air and
the stares of strangers.

Some say it's art,
the body as canvas, right of self expression,
preserved with pain to intensify the disclosure.
And what of the self? Devotion to God,
a memorial for a family, testament to love.
All the bonds that are tied in a person
even if the knots are loose.

People my age
have all those deep ties in the heart. The fires
of emotion not banked, the embers aglow.
Still a veil of caution thrown over raw feelings,
a sense of secrecy, intimacy clothed, unfit
for a stranger's eyes. There is also wonder
that this has been revealed and

curiosity about
a troubling reality which may lurk beneath
the bold surface of the skin, and why the unsealing
of the secret heart is so necessary. We old ones
look for reasons, some way to handle the strange
without touching the depths of our own defenses.

Larry in Limbo

for L.R. Robinson Jr.
who will never read this poem

When I was a child in parochial school,
the priests and nuns would tell us about
limbo, a state of suspended animation
for the souls of the innocent who were
not baptized, a consciousness suspended
between the life of heaven and the black
death of hell.

When my father-in-law began to mislay
his keys, his words and his way, the doctors
said that he was beginning to lose his
"executive function," a benign poultice
for his wounded wife. She thought that now
he would no longer bear the responsibilities
of a work-obsessed CEO.

No one prepared her for his steady descent
into early dementia. There were no soft words
available for the empty stare, the slack jaw,
the weakness in the legs, the permanent
acceptance of the walker, then the wheel chair,
the utter inability to use the executive bathroom
without help.

Soul and Spirit

Sun and water are the soul of the valley, the force
in the green vines, in the trees laden with fruit, the row crops,
the berries, even the weeds pushing through the cracked
concrete to sprout and grow. When I made my journey,
I knew nothing of this place, nothing of the life in the soil
nothing of the labor in the fields, nothing of the husbandry
that brought the valley to life.

        I knew the crash and clutter
of the city, the press of people, the random clang of cable
cars, the hiss of brakes as the bus wheezed to my stop.
I knew the frantic pace of business, even after the day was
done, and the lights still burned in the great buildings. Why
did I stay there? How many years went missing in a fever
of order and emptiness? An apartment, a desk, a routine that
made the dead day pass.

        When I came here
at last to the valley, it took time to sense the spirit of the place,
to engrave an understanding of the word "home," as a writer
finally finds words for something he knows he must say.
I had found a pathway to a place where I had no idea I would
ever live because the valley had no meaning in the glitter
of the city. No resonance. There was no lens through which
to see the dynamic angles alive in such an ordinary area.

        Is there any wonder
seen in the plate of peas on the dining room table, in the
juice that bursts from a nectarine when the knife bites? Any
grasp of the urge rising like divine fire from the seed through
the soil to the air? So easy to see miracles in the wizardry
of complex machines and ingenious devices, so difficult
in a pedestrian place where crops are sown and grown,
then sent to the city to be bought, cleaned and cooked, the
miracle of growth packaged on the shelf of a market.

Decline

Every day, it seems there's something
        old, some
body part we thought was working well
        and then
it wasn't, some wear and tear expected
        but not
an abrupt decline, sudden and unforeseen
        like the
stun blindness on the road to Damascus.
        Might be
we hear the voice of God, demanding that
        we stop
and consider, admit our frailty, finally cop
        to the
weakness of the flesh we were warned
        about by
our prophets in white lab coats probing,
        poking,
listening to the heartless throb of old
        age.
No sign of divinity there but we swear
        by them
and worship their knowledge of the nether
        world we
cannot travel. So when the voice is heard,
        we follow
or forebear. Just a few more miles, we say,
        as our
mothers promised, what we thought to
        claim
as our birthright, always there no matter
        what
risks we took on the long road or what
        monsters
we met and faced, fearless, on the way.

Worry

My wife worries, as she should,
so many changes, the past few years:
my balance harder to maintain;
difficult to keep safe footing after
tripping on a step or the cracked
concrete in the patio; arms and legs
scarred from scrapes against sharp
edges, heart medication making
blood flow at the slightest touch;
some fumbling with glasses, dishes,
after the evening meal and I try
to be helpful.

                There was a time
not long ago when I did so much
without thought, habitual patterns
which held my life together but now
such uncertainty: the spectre of a stroke,
cancer, heart attack, and on the horizon
the doom of dementia, a fear that some
blunders may mean more than just a
bother, so no sense of security; but
in spite of scraped skin or bruised feelings,
such an anguished effort to be in control
and preserve dignity.

Oskar

The day my dog was put to sleep
began like any other. Though now
half-blind, he could not hear, could
not control himself, a senile old
dog, the vet said, time he went
painlessly away, so first we walked,
like any other day, his hind legs
weak and shaking, but his nose still
busy, snuffling through the ivy border
near the street.

              On days like this,
I remember my mother, restrained
in her wheelchair, diapered, drugged,
eyes empty. No words. No touch as I
wheeled her to the patio, the son
who put her down there. Six years until
her plaque-tangled brain could not control
the vital organs. Six years of darkness
maintained so the feeble spark could
flicker. Six years in limbo, neither dead
nor alive, so her soul could be saved.
There was no last walk, no final chuck
behind the ears, just a phone call and
she was finally gone.

Old Age

You find yourself at a certain age
with sudden questions which build
and break, like waves on a lonely
shingle, moments of sadness, but
formless as sea spray, the cause
unknown: a former wife, an empty
job, children who are somehow
strangers, and in those moments
you may wonder what you could
have done or might have failed
to do.

              I remember my father,
standing for a moment by the ocean,
staring at the grey surge of water
heaving at the rocks: hypnotic tidal
rhythms, wind and wave. Could
he still see the shed in Poznan
where he was born and then ran from,
taste the scraps of grim potatoes that
were his daily meal, still smell the pigs
that he was made to tend?

                  And my
mother, resting on her bed in the afternoon,
staring at the ceiling, eyes open, then
getting up with a little laugh, bemused,
as if she could dismiss the disappointments
of her ordinary life and the promise
offered by her faith as consolation without,
as she would say, another word.

A Change of Seasons in the Sierra

Black clouds forming over Dodge Ridge this morning:
late June and the irony of early summer rainfall,
untimely, as the dog and I move through the trees.
Dry shafts of snow plants are dull in the meadow grass.
Clumps of yellow iris fade on the forest floor,
heads drooping, flat leaves showing brown at the tips.
Among the bones of fallen trees, the dog noses scattered
feathers, a bird caught by the rush of a sudden owl.

To the west, in a hospital bed two hundred miles away,
my friend lies dying, her hair a pale yellow on the pillow.
What consumes her is the insatiable love that nature holds,
the embrace of mortality, the steady passion that pulls us,
inevitably, into a pervasive aura enfolding the earth,
limitless as the purple spread of lupine across the Sierra,
dense as the mist which envelops the dog and me
as we walk on, closer each step, each moment to her.

Remember, friend, that dying begins with our first breath.
Seconds, minutes, cells trickle slowly, imperceptively away,
down to the sea, like Strawberry Creek in midsummer.
But a fresh torrent will rush through the canyon each spring.
Birds and buds will emerge from the chill death of winter,
the jays will move in a blue flutter through the trees, and the
snow plants in May will thrust passionately through the soil.
In pools of sunlight, the slender iris will sway in the meadow.

Degeneration

When we are born, it begins, the slow
slide of cells toward a final end. Unfelt
in our youth, the changes so subtle,
disarming and veiled that in old age
we are surprised when the signs begin
to appear, when organs and limbs no
longer can be trusted: delusions, we
hope, seen through a cloudy lens.

        Surely, this mortality was
known; we must have been aware, but
were we too captivated, luxuriating in
the beauty of our young bodies, flesh firm,
eyes bright, brain attentive? Was there not
some soft call from the spirit that whispered
the truth but went unheard in our hubris?

        The woman who was yet
to be my wife was never touched by injury
or illness, and when she stood before me
in her nakedness, I could not imagine her
otherwise, blinded by her beauty, could not
foresee the changes that she would bear.
Her life force flowed. So did mine. Believing.

Agony of Death

The agony of death lurks in the mind
as the depth of the void begins to be seen,
and questions arise about the end and
the form it will follow. My mother was a
woman of faith, but still filled with dread.
"Pray that you make a good death," she
would tell me, but how will my good death
be made? For her, she imagined a priest,
unctious smear of oil on her forehead,
a last confession, hands folded on the coverlet,
light going quietly out of the eyes. But that
comfort will not be mine.

                Physical agony is
another matter, a sharper snap, no balm
for spiritual anxiety, just relief from torment
of the body: enough morphine to dull
the piercing throb, a sedative to sooth
the mind, together a release from the pain
that darkens the light, allows no other focus,
even for the most profound of questions,
as the organs slip slowly into waste, and the
mind can no longer manage. Without the
faith of my mother I can only accept the
end of the spark and hope that this fiction
will be concluded in peace.

Solitude

As some of us age, our search for the soul
        becomes urgent;
embers banked for years begin to glow
        and we know
that the unctious sermons of pastors
        are not enough.

All true wisdom, say the shamans, is only
        found in the vast
solitude and can be acquired only through
        suffering and privation,
by a journey toward meaning at the end of
        days, following the call

of the spirit, a road seldom taken in an
        occupied life, filled
with the busyness of everyday clatter:
        solitary travel without
rest at a welcoming inn, small talk or the
        comfort of congregations.

We take a long walk alone on a trail or
        find a seat overlooking
the endless expanse of the ocean and
        allow ourselves
to question what may lie in the dark,
        unknown territory

ahead, and when we come to the end
        of this difficult
journey and arrive at the presence
        of the spirit,
what do we find? The settled quiet
        that lovers

come to after the blessing of many years
        together, walking
on a beach, sharing a meal: the peace
        of contented rest
and acceptance of the final silence when
        all is answered.

Simple Prayer

The old man walks across the street to the nursery,
buys a flat of impatiens, mixed colors, seated in
small plastic containers. Why choose this time to
plant?

        It's early April and the ground
is warm in the bright sunshine. He's prepared the
soil, mixed in a little fertilzer of the old kind,
steer manure,

        and he wants somehow to sanctify this
season in the valley. All around him trees are leafing
out, bees busy in the budding flowers, and he feels
that the earth

        is waiting for him to pray, to kneel
in the dirt, press the plants into the soil, smell the
pungent scent of humus rising as he breaks up the
ground

        and plants the seedlings. He's an old man,
and this act of worship is hard on his knees, hard
on his back but he does not know a better way
to honor

        creation as he is dying which is not a final
sentence, but a phrase which tolls the beginning
from his first breath and then an ending in the winter
ground.

Balance

Difficult when I step from one
      year to another,
each bringing me closer to an
      end which was
once a vague shimmer in the
      distance, like a
mirage in the desert, but is now
      clear on the
horizon as the sun begins to set.

Of course, it is now that balance
      is so important:
one misstep on a slippery sidewalk,
      one fall from a
stool while reaching too high and
      then Prompt Care
to wait for a doctor and an even
      longer wait while
the broken bone heals and sets.

Sometimes it's not a bone that
      is broken but a bond
with a child who has a heart you
      are sure you can
heal, so you stretch yourself
      further and higher
than you know you should,
      beyond the limits
that you and the child have set.

The young pay little for losing
      their balance: a few
bruises, a few scrapes, a new
      job, a new wife,
rehab, and some years to find
      firm footing. The
old lack that insolent prosperity
      so they try to hold
their ground as the sun sets.

Old Ball Game

It's the last of the seventh and the starting
pitcher is still in. He has good velocity and
a sharp break on the curve, but he misses
his spots, occasionally, and he seems to
be tiring.

The set-up man, in the bullpen, has been
steady all year. The eighth inning has been
his, and he throws strikes, always low and
away on the corners, great command and
no one ever walks.

The closer is a mystery; you never know
what to expect. He starts you out with two
fast balls, taken for strikes on the corner,
then a slider with a nasty break. You swing
weakly. Game over.

Miracles

Simple miracles are everywhere around us,
if we choose to look, shining and common:
a pond brilliant in dappled light, the grandeurs
of even familiar flowers, and when we are
stunned by the vast civilizations found in
sun and water, how can we not stop for
a moment and try to comprehend?

                              Of course,
reflection is not given to all nor prized,
often deflected for the sadness it is thought
to hold. We see the tree burdened with the
brilliant leaves in autumn it is soon to shed
and find sorrow there for the beauty that
will turn to mulch in a month, not seeing
the intricacy of the turning world, the wonder
of that whirl.

                    My mother was a simple
person, humbled by her presence in the world,
wanting only a place for her soul in the final
mystery. Yet she would stand by the window
overlooking the ocean and look out toward the
horizon to see the last flash of the fading sun
as it dropped below the edge of the world.

What might have occurred to her, stunned
by the beauty of the clouds, the last gasp
of the dying day? Was she able to connect
that intricate moment with her own fragility
as she watched that beautiful ruin?

The Body Politic

My wife says that my body is changing,
               trousers slack
in the rear, buttocks frail and formless,
               the flesh falling
away, the deficit uncontrollable. Now
               it's just a matter
of waiting for The Big One: heart attack,
               cancer, the fiscal
cliff or another war. There's nothing further
               to be done,
resolutions made and enacted: all that
               biking and walking,
a careful diet, but no way now to govern
               a body falling slowly
into decline. It does not seem so long ago
               that the state
of my body was sound, several surgeries
               to be sure,
but always the muscles regaining their tone
               and tension.
Now this gradual recession, and no renewal
               seems possible,
every glance in the mirror a reflection of the loss.

About the Author

PAUL NEUMANN was born and raised on the coast of California. For the past forty-six years he has made his home in Modesto with his wife, Pamela. Following his retirement from MJC, he became a serious and disciplined poet. His first book, *"Forms of Light,"* was published in 2003. His second collection, *"This Valley,"* appeared in 2013 and was informed by his love for the land and the people. in the Central Valley. This latest collection, *"Beginnings and Endings,"* begins with a series of poems inspired by the birth of his granddaughter, Mary. The last segment of the book examines issues of aging, a subject influenced by his own mortality.

QUERCUS
Review
P R E S S